Eastern Grey Kangaroo in full flight.

KANGAROOS

The world's largest living marsupials, and Australia's best known, are the great Kangaroos, including the Reds of inland plains, the Greys of southern forests and bushlands and the Antilopine Kangaroo of tropical grasslands.

In the days of early exploration of Australia, it was thought that the young of Kangaroos were actually born in the mother's pouch, however later investigation revealed this to be incorrect. They are incredibly small at birth (newborn Red Kangaroos are only approx. 18mm. long), blind and immature, but immediately after birth, claw their way unaided through the fur to the mother's pouch. Here they attach themselves to a teat and remain nourished and growing in the warm pouch for at least six months.

Family name for the Kangaroo is the elongated hind feet, and was first applied in 1790 to the Great Grey. The hind legs with long powerful feet, permit great speed in long leaping bounds of up to 10m. Specialization of the hind legs and rejection of the fore-limbs for speedy travel produced a perfectly balanced action with the great pendulum tail acting as balancer and rudder.

Over the ages, the teeth of these gentle herbivores modified and became ideal for their vegetarian diet. Maximum sizes of Kangaroos are hard to authenticate, but in the Australian Museum the largest Grey is 2.64m. Maximum age of Kangaroos in the wild is impossible to estimate, but teeth tests of some in captivity reveal upper limits from 15-22 years. An interesting feature of Kangaroos is their continued growth into old age.

A powerfully built male Red Kangaroo.

Red Kangaroo.

Kangaroo Island Kangaroo.

Female Red Kangaroo with Joey.

Young Western Grey Kangaroo.

New-born Joey.

5

Eastern Grey male Kangaroo.

Eastern Grey female Kangaroo with inquisitive Joey.

Male Red Kangaroo.

Female Red Kangaroo with Joey.

RED KANG
(Photograph

S WITH SMALLER AGILE WALLABY. BENNETT'S WALLABY IN THE FOREGROUND.
Bimbimbie Wildlife Park).

Sandy or Agile Wallaby.

WALLABIES

Except for Rock Wallabies and Tree Kangaroos, there are very few outward differences between most Wallabies and Kangaroos, other than size and markings; the Red-necked Wallaby is often mistaken for a Kangaroo. The distinguishing characteristics of Wallabies are the smaller foot length which ranges from 164mm. to 254mm., and the smaller skull; also range of habitat is greater than that of the Kangaroo, probably because they choose to live in more densely vegetated country, with the smaller Wallabies preferring thick undergrowth for their home.

The colourful Rock Wallaby which inhabits rough country and rocky out-crops throughout Australia, also occurs on small rocky islands around the coast, but is not found in Tasmania. Pademelons are very small Wallabies wich live among thickets and undergrowth. These shy little marsupials have become very rare — to the point of extinction — in many of their mainland territories; mainly due to the imported predatory fox, dingoes and the alarming population explosion of feral cats. In Tasmania, where there is absence of foxes and dingoes, the Pademelon is still plentiful.

Although the fate of many of these smaller marsupials is now very much in the balance, one occasionally re-appears when thought to be extinct. The rare Parma Wallaby, last sighted in the Dorrigo district in 1932, was re-discovered in 1965 on Kawau Island off the coast of New Zealand where it had been introduced in the 1870s then forgotten. Coincidentally, this distinctive Wallaby soon afterwards was found near Gosford, New South Wales.

Black-tailed Wallaby.

Group of Pretty-faced Wallabies.

Tammar Wallaby.

Black-striped Wallaby.

Bennett's Wallabies.

Parma Wallaby.

Red-necked Pademelon.

Quokka or Short-tailed Pademelon.

Yellow-footed Rock Wallaby.

13

Male & female Euros.

WALLAROOS

The name "Wallaroo", derived from the Aboriginal "Wolaru", was originally applied to all larger Kangaroos of eastern New South Wales, but has since been restricted to the smaller robust rock-dwelling Kangaroos of all States.

Wallaroos are widely distributed over the mainland and live among the rocky haunts of coastal ranges and inland ridges. As befits their rocky environment, they have comparatively short and stocky hind legs suited to leaping among rocks, and their broad feet have roughened soles to prevent slipping. They are perfectly adapted to the rocky slopes and gullies and are almost impossible to capture whilst in their home environment. The males are determined fighters, using their strong teeth and nails as well as their great muscular power.

Although immediately recognizable by heavy build and shaggy fur, nevertheless, because of their wide distribution

Wallaroos are subject to considerable local variation and some hybridism. However, all have the distinguishing muzzle tip entirely hairless between the nostrils and also an extraordinarily broad upper third incisor tooth.

A unique member of the Macropodidae family which warrants mention is the Tree Kangaroo. These interesting animals have undergone a secondary phase of evolution. Although all Kangaroos originally descended from primitive tree-dwelling stock adapting to their earth-bound existence very successfully, this particular member reverted to the trees, with marked physical changes necessary to the altered environment. Although ungainly on land, they are amazingly agile in the trees, making great leaps of over 9m. They are essentially forest-loving creatures and the two mainland species (now endangered) are restricted to tropical north-east Queensland

Wallaroo with Joey.